E
SIM

Simon, Norma

What do I say?

DATE		
	DE 18 '91	MR 28 '96
MAY 18 '82	MR 04 '92	MAY 09
OC 13 '83	OC 15 '92	
SE 12 '85	AP 08 '93	
JA 29 '87	AP 28 '93	
JA 27 '89	OC 14 '93	
FE 28 '90	NO 04 '93	
OC 24 '90	SE 07 '94	
MR 01 '91	NO 08 '94	
NO 06 '91	MR 02 '95	
	MR 20 '96	

© THE BAKER & TAYLOR CO.

What Do I Say?

Story: **NORMA SIMON**   Pictures: **JOE LASKER**

ALBERT WHITMAN & Company   Chicago

This Book is dedicated
by the Author and Artist
to Caroline

Text © 1967 by Norma Simon. Illustrations © 1967 by Joe Lasker.
Library of Congress Catalog Card 67-17420
Published simultaneously in Canada by General Publishing, Limited, Toronto
Lithographed in the United States of America
Third Printing 1980
This book is available in an English/Spanish Edition.

A Note to Those Who Use This Book with Children . . .

Wherever I visit, my attention is inevitably drawn to children—what they do and what they say. Children everywhere have so much in common. Some children have more to say than others, but, with encouragement, all of them want to make contact with people, to let people know who they are.

In the towns and cities all over our country there are small boys like the child in our story. He enjoys his world because it is warm and secure for him and because he knows no other world. The child's day is reflected in his own terms and his own words.

When your listeners hear you read this book, we hope that they will say "Just like me" aloud or to themselves. And, as they become involved in each situation and anticipate and say aloud the responses of the boy in the story, your listeners become "readers," too.

Manuel, the little boy in this story, is a Puerto Rican child in a large American city, but every child can make this his own story. No matter if the children's words differ from the text, as long as they wish to participate in the telling. If adults can help children feel how very personal a book can be, they can help provide the first key insights that open the door to reading.

NORMA SIMON

I get up in the morning.

What do I say?

I drink my milk.

What do I say?

All done!

I play with Baby.

What do I say?

Peek-a-boo!

I leave my baby home.

What do I say?

Bye-bye.

I open the door.

What do they say?

Hi!

Teacher says, "What's your name?"

What do I say?

I'm Manuel.

Teacher says, "How do you do?"

"My name is Mrs. Booth."

What's your name?

I talk on the
telephone.

What do I say?

Hello!

See what I have.

What do I say?

Let's play.

Something for me?

What do I say?   Thank you.

Something's wrong.

What do I say?

Please help me.

I want to swing.

What do I say?   It's my turn.

Oh, oh! I bump somebody.

What do I say?

Excuse me.

Time to go home.

What do we say?

So long!

I like this.   What do I say?

More, please.

I wash my face.   I brush my teeth.

What do I say?   All ready for bed.

I jump in my bed.

What do I say?

Good-night!

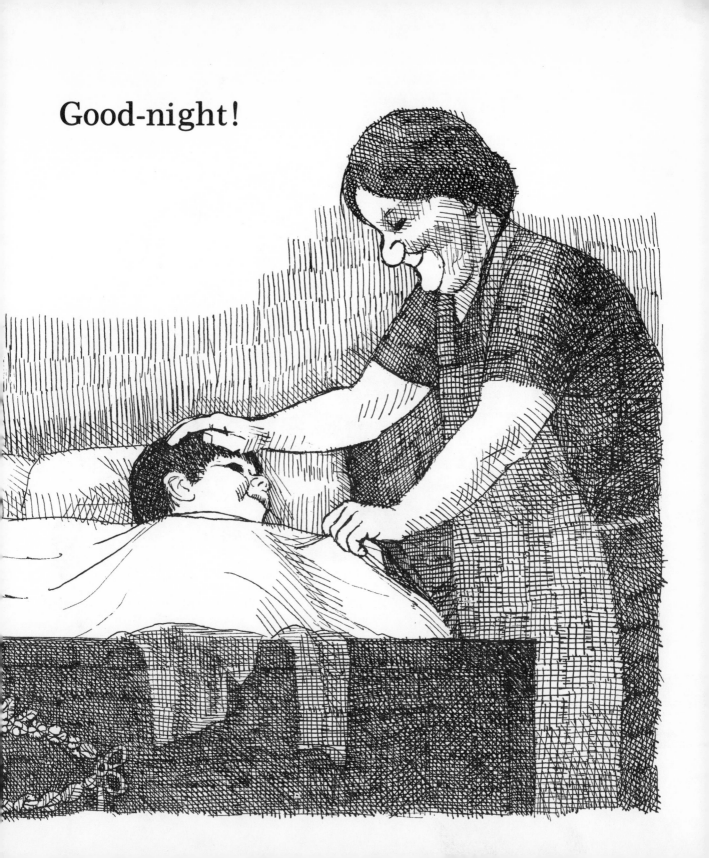